CRAFT & CRITIQUE SERIES, BOOK 1

Giving and Receiving Effective Critique

THE CRITIQUE DOCTOR'S GUIDE TO HELPING OTHER WRITERS WRITE BETTER (AND STILL BE YOUR FRIENDS)

ROSS LAMPERT
(A.K.A. THE CRITIQUE DOCTOR)

Giving and Receiving Effective Critique
Copyright © 2025 by Ross Lampert (a.k.a. The Critique Doctor).

NO AI TRAINING

Without in any way limiting the author's and publisher's exclusive rights under copyright, any use of this publication to "train" generative artificial intelligence (AI) technologies to generate text is expressly prohibited. The author reserves all rights to license uses of this work for generative AI training and development of machine learning language models.

All rights reserved. No part of this book may be reproduced or transmitted in any form or by any means, electronic or mechanical, including photocopying, recording, or by any information storage and retrieval system, without permission in writing from the copyright owner.

This book was printed in the United States of America.

Paperback ISBN: 978-0-9897251-6-3

Book Cover Design and Interior Formatting by 100Covers.

DEDICATION

This book—indeed the entire Craft & Critique series—is dedicated to you, the writer who not only wants to improve your own work but to help other writers improve theirs.

Contents

Series Introduction ix
Introduction to This Book xvii

Chapter 1: Giving Effective Critique: Preparation,
            First Steps, and the Author 1
Chapter 2: Delivering Your Critique 23

Appendices
Appendix 1: Critique Guides 41
Appendix 2: Cochise Writers' Group Expectations Document 53

ACKNOWLEDGMENTS

So many friends and writers have contributed to this series since it began as a set of blog posts in 2011 that it's impossible to name them all. If you're one of them, please know that I am deeply grateful for your ideas, suggestions, and critiques, even the ones that had some sharp edges to them.

Katie Chambers of Beacon Point Services did
yeoman's work editing these books.
100 Covers created the covers.
Author photo by Caitlin Ebbing, Caitlin Ebbing Photography.

Series Introduction

What This Series Will Teach You

Let's cut right to the chase: giving good critique is something most people have to learn how to do. Closely reading a work—whether fiction, nonfiction, a script, or poetry—and assessing its strengths and weaknesses is not natural for most of us. Sure, starting in grade school, our English teachers tried to teach us how to do it. Unfortunately, for many students, that also sucked the joy out of reading and turned it into drudgery and hard work.

Nevertheless, some of us retained an urge to create, to write either for our own pleasure or for others to read. And a few brave souls decided that for their work to get better, they needed feedback, not just from teachers but from other active writers, people who were ahead of them in their development and could offer tips and suggestions on how to make their words come alive on the page.

But as I said, giving good (or effective) critique is neither easy nor natural. So that's what this series is about: helping you learn how to give that good critique. In the process, you'll also learn how to evaluate your own work and make it better before you give it to someone else for their review.

The Difference between Critique and Criticism

"Criticism" has two meanings. The first one is finding fault. This often comes laden with negative emotions and, at its worst, can be spirit crushing.

The second meaning, literary criticism, is the kind of "expert" analysis done by English professors and others whose job it is to "look under the hood" of a work and evaluate its content, structure, meaning, etc.

Literary criticism has its parallels in all the creative arts: music, painting, sculpture, theater, television and movies, dance, even architecture.

While "critique" relates to both of these meanings, it is not either one of them. Critique does have the job of identifying what didn't work in a piece, but its purpose is to help the author fix the problem. Critique should also identify what the author did well so they can repeat that success. *How* the review is done and presented also matters: it needs to be honest but as helpful and constructive as possible. Trashing a work doesn't help the author. Neither does sugarcoating or avoiding discussing problems.

Critique is also different from literary criticism in that critique happens while a work is being developed. Literary criticism, on the other hand, happens only after the work has been completed and published.

In short, a critique is a thoughtful, thorough, constructive analysis of a work in progress. It aims to help the writer write better.

Why I've Written This Series

I've been involved in critique groups off and on since I was in college in the mid-1970s. However, I really focused on them while I was getting a Master of Arts degree in English (with a creative writing specialization) in the mid-2000s at the University of Central Oklahoma. After I got the degree and moved to Arizona, I joined a local writers' group, but became dissatisfied with how they worked. Another member of the group and I decided to form one of our own that approached critique differently, and so the Cochise Writers' Group was born in 2007.

In 2012, the members of the group and I put together a list of questions we thought we should ask ourselves as we reviewed each piece. That list turned into a series of blog posts I put on my website. I updated them starting in 2018, but I didn't feel that was enough: there needed to be a book. Those revised posts formed the basis for what started as one book, but grew and grew until I had to break it up into this series. The latest versions of those posts are on The Critique Doctor website (https://thecritiquedoctor.com/).

The Critique Doctor

What's in This Series

The series is made up of six books:

- Book 0, *Finding the Write Fit* (https://books2read.com/u/mYO8wY) is a guide for evaluating one or more in-person critique groups, social media–based groups, or online critique sites to find one that's a good fit for you. It also provides an overview of online and in-person courses and classes that aren't associated with a college or university, looks at artificial intelligence applications as potential critique tools, and guides you through the process of forming your own in-person group if you decide you aren't comfortable with any of the other options. Since it *is* a kind of prequel—you can't give and receive critique from other writers unless you're in some kind of critique relationship with them—I'm calling it Book 0. If you're already a member of a critique group or site, that book can still help if you aren't completely satisfied with it and are looking for pointers on how to fix it or find a better one.

Finding the Write Fit

- This book is about what the title says it is: preparing you to give effective critique, based on the approaches and techniques I'll teach in the other books, and to evaluate the critiques you receive.
- Book 2, *Mechanics, Narrative, and Description* (https://books2read.com/u/4NOogJ), provides tools for evaluating an author's use of the mechanics of writing: spelling, grammar, punctuation, and capitalization. Then it digs into narrative, the text outside of quotation

Mechanics, Narrative, and Description

marks, and description, in setting, characterization, and other areas.

- Book 3, *Theme, Plot, and Structure* (https://books2read.com/u/mdOjqd), looks at those topics and much more: the beginnings and endings of scenes, chapters, and whole books; what theme, plot, and structure are and how they work together; how stakes, conflict, tension, and pace are woven into a story—or should be—and how to tell if the writer is handling all these topics well.

Theme, Plot, and Structure

- Book 4, *Characters and Dialogue* (https://books2read.com/u/mYOzkM), covers all the aspects of the people or other beings who populate our books: their roles, how they're portrayed, and how they communicate with each other.

Characters and Dialogue

- Book 5, *Poetry Critique for Prose Writers* (https://books2read.com/u/mB6QqN), will demystify the processes of reading, understanding, and critiquing poems. If you're a member of an in-person group, or join one later, it's a good bet that at some time you'll be asked to review someone's poetry. For many prose writers, this can be an intimidating request. This book will help you overcome that feeling. And who knows, you might even discover that you *like* poetry!

Poetry Critique for Prose Writers

Each book also contains appendices with helpful tools and information that didn't fit comfortably in the text.

Why the Series Is Organized the Way It Is

That nice, neat structure for the books and chapters to come is true and correct... sort of. But the truth is, many of those topics overlap. For example, the techniques of showing and telling apply to plot, characterization, and setting. Dialogue is a great way to reveal character, create conflict and tension, and even provide setting details.

So in many ways, the structure of the series is arbitrary. It is not, however, capricious. I've put a lot of thought into which topics go into which book—but with the full knowledge that they often apply to other books too. I'll do what I can to make that clear throughout, and even repeat necessary material between the books.

How to Use These Books, and How Not To

What I'm about to say may surprise you. While, yes, you should read *this* book all the way through, I *do not* recommend that for the next four. Why in the world would I do that?

It's pretty simple: there's simply too much information in Books 2 – 5, especially 2 – 4, for you to absorb. I'm not saying that because I think poorly of you. I'm saying it because that's the feedback I've gotten from my critique group and other readers. Their brains exploded, and that's not a pretty sight.

So instead of reading them from cover to cover, treat those books as if they were encyclopedias or wikis. Use them when you're looking for suggestions on how to address a specific problem you've come across in a work you're reviewing. Maybe the author's dialogue is stiff and stilted. There's an article on that. Or they've provided too little setting detail, or too much. There are articles on those topics. And so on.

The concept is similar to Angela Ackerman's and Becca Puglisi's nine-book Writers Helping Writers series [https://www.amazon.com/dp/B07ZH6WS6C] (The Emotion Thesaurus [https://books2read.com/u/bwGeMY], The Conflict Thesaurus [https://books2read.com/u/baM18a], etc.), which I highly recommend.

Writers Helping Writers   The Emotion Thesaurus   The Conflict Thesaurus

In addition, almost every article in Books 2 – 5 ends with a series of questions you can use to help you zero in on exactly what the problem is and to give you ideas on what you can recommend to the author so they can overcome it. These books, and The Critique Doctor website (https://thecritiquedoctor.com/) which supports them, are a toolkit for you to use whenever you need it.

The Critique Doctor

The whole idea is to give you the kind of targeted, focused advice that will help you give the best possible guidance to your fellow writers. That's what good critique is, after all, and that's what this series is about.

And remember, the tools you use to help provide effective critique are just as valuable when you're editing your own work. Maybe even more so.

> **NOTE: Throughout these books I will use the words "critiquer" and "reviewer" interchangeably, even though a reviewer typically does not provide feedback directly to the author, nor are they commenting on a work that's still in development. However, in the context of this series, the words carry the same meaning.**

All right. That's enough about the series as a whole. Now let me introduce you to this book.

Introduction to This Book

A famous writer, possibly W. Somerset Maugham, supposedly said, "There are three rules of writing. Unfortunately, nobody knows what they are." This is true about critique too. But I want you to focus on the word "rules," not the number.

Critique of a work in progress (a WIP) is *not* about making that work perfect—a fool's errand if there ever was one—but about helping the author grow as a writer, to expand their knowledge of the craft. As anyone who's been writing for any length of time knows, there's *always* more to learn, and how we approach a particular element of a story is going to vary every time we do it. And that's true of every writer we offer our feedback to.

There are no rules about how to do critique, and anyone who tells you there are is lying. Or doesn't know what they're talking about.

So instead of rules, this book offers a set of suggestions and guides, based on my years of experience giving and receiving critique and that of the writers I've worked with and studied. These suggestions have stood the test of time but are general enough that they can be applied broadly—or ignored in whole or in part, which is necessary sometimes.

But while the guidelines are general, they often need to be applied specifically, that is, to a specific moment or place in a piece. That's the balance I've tried to strike throughout.

Chapter 1, on giving effective critique, is a top-level view of the process of critiquing: what your goals should be as a reviewer, the different kinds of critique, and the differences between what I call "technique" and "procedure."

Chapter 2 discusses how to deliver your critique, especially how to think about the other person in the critique equation—the author. While providing clear and honest feedback is central to giving good critique, tact is also important. Mark Twain defined tact as "the art of telling a man to go to Hell in such a way as to make him eager to begin the journey." While I doubt you'll be telling your fellow author *that*, you could very well come across a piece that, shall we say, needs a lot of work. (There's an example of tact for you, although it's not an effective critique since it doesn't offer any suggestions of what changes the piece would benefit from.) You know how you'd feel if someone told you your "baby" was butt-ugly. You can be sure the person sitting across the table from you or at the other end of a Zoom call would feel the same way. *Good* critique helps the author improve their weak areas and makes them eager to get to work doing so. And you should feel the same way if a critique is delivered well to you.

But enough with the introducing, already! Let's get to work.

Chapter 1

Giving Effective Critique: Preparation, First Steps, and the Author

If you're in any kind of critique-giving and -receiving relationship, whether it's one-on-one with another writer, in a creative writing class, or as part of an in-person or online writers' or critique group or website, how you give—and take—critique matters. When you're reviewing someone else's work, *how* you say it is just as important as what you say. And when you're receiving feedback, how you respond to it determines how willing your critique partners are to give you honest evaluations in the future.

That's why everyone should read this chapter all the way through. Let me say that again.

Everyone should read this chapter all the way through.

Effective critiquing involves knowing:

- What effective critique is
- The difference between "technique" and "procedure" in critique
- How to read when critiquing a work
- The tools critiquers need to be effective, especially if you're a new critiquer, and the techniques to avoid
- When and how to give praise (and when and how not to)
- Some special considerations if you're reviewing a first draft

Ready? Let's get started.

What Is Effective Critique?

New critiquers almost always say, "I don't know how to critique." If that's you, you're in luck: that's what this part of the chapter is all about. In fact, it's what the whole series is about. I suspect new reviewers tend to think they have to do what they did in high school or college English classes: identify and explain the symbolism in a passage, say, or compare and contrast the use of metaphor with onomatopoeia.

Nope! Nope, nope, nope. As I suggested in the introductions, even if you enjoyed those classes and that kind of analysis, that's not the feedback you'll give or receive in a critique group or site.

The core of effective critique is helping the author get better by identifying what worked, what didn't, and why; how the author might improve what's not working; and how to build on what they did well. That means:

The critique must be honest, specific, and constructive.

It must *not*, however, be an attempt to rewrite the author's work. You, the reviewer, must always keep in mind that it's *their* work, not yours. This is an easy trap to fall into, especially since the differences between being helpful and taking over the piece to make it fit your particular style or preferences can be subtle. I'll say more about this *see page 15*.

Since it can be hard to see the distinction, author and creative writing instructor Eric Witchey has even suggested *authors* train their reviewers on how to critique *them*, in part by telling those readers up front their goals for the story. "Story" here means *any* piece of creative writing, from flash fiction or poetry at the short end, through chapters in a book or acts in a script, to a full-length work. This includes memoir and both creative and functional nonfiction too.

An author's goals include far more than where and when they hope to sell the book. They include how the writer wants the reader to react to the piece, and for scenes, chapters, and acts, how those components are supposed to move the story forward in terms of plot *and* characterization.

Giving and Receiving Effective Critique

In an article on Writershelpingwriters.net (https://tinyurl.com/yc7wkhwt), script consultant Michael Hauge listed five things highly effective critique group members do:

Writers Helping Writers

1. They ask questions, specifically about how the author envisions their story and characters. This is good to do when the group first encounters a story, but it could also be very worthwhile later, especially if the story—or the author—is losing steam or seems to have strayed from its original intent.
2. They listen carefully to the author's answers, digging for what lies underneath their words. We're already doing this with *our* characters, right? So why not listen like this with our fellow group members?
3. With those questions and answers in hand, they point out where the story doesn't align with the author's vision for it. Or where the reader lost interest in the story. But the key piece of this step is for the reviewer to explain *why* that happened, as best they can.
4. Now they can offer suggestions on how to fix the problems they found. Sometimes that means doing nothing more than asking, "What if... ?" and letting things develop from there.
5. Finally, the author also listens carefully before responding. But responding does not mean defending or arguing. The former isn't necessary; the latter isn't productive. It's fair for the author to point out if they feel the reader missed or misunderstood something important or to ask if anyone else reacted the same way to that point. That question might not be necessary if the author waits, or isn't allowed to speak, until everyone else has had their say. If several group members had the same or a similar reaction, that should come out in the discussion. The author can also propose their own ideas in response to those comments—"What if I tried this... ?" or "What if the character said/did this... ?"—to see how the group reacts. Ultimately, the decision on whether to change anything at all, or what to change, is the author's, but the group's insights and different perspectives can be very helpful.

So long as everyone in the group—author and critiquers alike—is focused on helping each work get better, discussions like these can only be good.

Critique, Technique, and Procedure

Read books, magazines, blogs, websites, you-name-it on writing and you'll be inundated, absolutely overwhelmed, with tips, tricks, hints, suggestions, ideas, and more on how to write everything from a poem to the Great American Novel, how to overcome writer's block, how to spur your creativity, how to... well, do just about anything and everything. Some writers, agents, or publishers will even insist you *must* follow their advice.

Bunk!

When I was in the Air Force, I was an instructor in my aircrew position on the E-3 Airborne Warning and Control System aircraft for a while. Part of my instructor training included learning the difference between "procedure" and "technique." Procedures were things we had to follow exactly as written in various documents because if we didn't, we could break expensive pieces of equipment or hurt people we didn't mean to. I could grade my students on how well they performed the one right way to do these procedures. (For those of you who've never been in the military, fewer of these procedures exist than the stereotypes would have you believe.)

"Technique," on the other hand, was everything else. Emphasis on *everything*. If we had more than one way to accomplish a task safely, on time, and without violating any established rules, regulations, or procedures, then any of those alternative ways were acceptable. As an instructor, I could critique my students on their technique and discuss alternatives, but I couldn't grade them on their performance, as long as the job got done as needed, when needed.

That's the way writing and critiquing are, only more so: 99.9 percent technique. It's a craft, after all, not engineering (with apologies to Larry Brooks, author of *Story Engineering*).

Even the "rules" about grammar, spelling, punctuation, capitalization, and so on are bendable if not completely breakable, particularly in fiction and poetry. (We'll still spend a lot of time on these rules in Book 2 [https://books2read.com/u/4NOogJ] and Book 5 [https://books2read.com/u/mB6QqN].) That bending or breaking needs to be done with intent, though, with a specific purpose in mind other than just "breaking the rules," but that makes the point.

Mechanics, Narrative, and Description

Poetry Critique for Prose Writers

Simply deciding to break or ignore a "rule"—for an extreme example, deciding not to use any punctuation—because doing so seems clever or outrageous is not a good reason to do it. For one thing, it's probably been done before by someone who actually knew what they were doing, and why. For another, if it makes the piece hard, even impossible to read, no one outside the group will ever want to read it. These rules exist for good reasons, like ensuring the reader can understand the work. The writer's creative use of them is technique.

Same goes for how you provide critique: you have lots of ways to do it. Some are better than others, depending on the situation. In other words, they're technique.

If there's one thing that *is* a rule, a "procedure," it's this:

Evaluate the writING, do not criticize the writER.

Said another way, evaluate the work, not the worker.

Reading to Critique

This is where the fun begins, when you get to start analyzing the work.

Not Reading for Pleasure

And right away, I'm going to throw you a curveball.

One of the hardest things for new reviewers to wrap their minds around is the fact that as a reviewer, they're not reading for pleasure. Ugh, that sounds like we're going back to English class, doesn't it? Well, yeah, we are, kind of. Sorry!

But here's the thing:

> **It doesn't matter whether you enjoy a piece or not.**
> **Your job is to evaluate whether it does**
> **what the author intended it to do:**
> **to entertain, inform, advocate, etc.**

If you happen to enjoy the piece while you're reading it, that's great. The author will appreciate knowing that.

But it's also possible to *not* enjoy a story—not enjoy it at all—and still see that it's well written. Let me give you an example.

A former member of my group wrote a draft novel about a highly dysfunctional young couple in Phoenix, Arizona. They had all sorts of things working against them: they didn't have a lot of money, were often unemployed or under-employed, had no meaningful support system to fall back on, and regularly made bad decisions. Perfect material for a certain kind of novel.

I didn't hate the story, but I certainly didn't enjoy reading it. At the same time, though, I had to acknowledge the author had done an excellent job crafting it. It was richly detailed, full of conflict and tension, the characters were well and clearly drawn, the dialogue was sharp and on-target, and the plot moved inexorably forward, with things getting worse and worse for the young couple and their baby.

It did all the things a novel should do—and did them well. It was just not a book I would have ever picked up on my own, and if I had, I would not have read it all the way through.

As a reviewer, you *will* encounter work like that. You don't like it? Tough cookies. Not the kind of work you read? Read it anyway. That author put a lot of time and effort into creating it. Now it's your obligation to give it the best kind of honest, thoughtful, constructive evaluation you can. The shoe *will* be on the other foot someday, maybe someday soon. This is the social contract you have in an in-person critique group, including one that's virtual (using a video conferencing app like Zoom) or hybrid (one that's both in person and virtual at the same time).

With the purely online critique sites, you can pick and choose which submissions to review, so you're less likely to read all the way through a piece you don't enjoy. That said, if you encounter a piece that isn't your thing, but you give it an honest, constructive review, that might encourage others to review the work you submit.

So if you aren't reading for pleasure, what *are* you reading for?

I'm glad you asked. While we'll dig *a lot* deeper into that, and how to do it, in the rest of the books in this series, you can ask a few questions about a piece every time you critique another writer's work.

Four Overall Questions

As you're reviewing a work, you'll want to ask and answer the following four questions.

#1: What didn't work, and what did? I know this seems like an odd question but many elements of a piece can succeed or come up short. They're the topics of the rest of the series. Not all of them will appear in every piece—at least, let's hope not! You're going to be on the lookout for all of them, though, and when you find one, your brain should go *ping*! (or *ah-ha*! or *uh-oh*!). That's when you'll move on to the next question.

#2: Where did it happen? Be specific! Identify the spot right on the manuscript. Do more than just underline or circle it, though. In your notes in the margin, on a separate sheet of paper, or in a word processor's or website's comment box, answer the next two questions.

#3: What was the exact nature of the problem or success?

Again, be as specific as possible.

WARNING
This requires actually *thinking* about the writing,
not just letting it go in one eye and out the other!

Seriously, this is a very writerly task, and it's a learned skill, which is what this series will help you do. If it takes you some time to learn it, that's OK.

One technique I use is to read each work twice. The first time, I read fairly quickly, just to get an overall sense of the piece. The second time is when I really slow down and look for the kinds of things these books will discuss.

As you learn how to do this kind of review, you'll find yourself applying it to your own writing as well, and that's the most powerful benefit of critiquing other people's work.

#4: What can the author do to fix the problem or repeat the success?

Another tough question! This one's tricky, though, because it's *not* your task to (re)write someone else's piece to fit your style. *(see page 15.)* Instead of saying, "If I was writing this story, I would have written…," go back to Question #3, see if you can determine what the writer was trying to accomplish, and then propose a way they might do it. They may or may not accept your suggestion, or they might come up with a different idea, thanks to your input.

Probably the best way to find out what the author meant to do is to ask. Yeah, OK, so I've got a blinding grasp of the obvious. But *is* that so obvious? Maybe it's so obvious we don't usually think of it. Or you may both discover that the author hadn't actually thought about it. This is probably most true for new writers and "pantsers," writers who build their first draft "by the seat of their pants." Experienced writers know that pretty much everything in their work must be put there with a specific purpose in mind, so asking this question may result in some revelations.

Learning how to help the author overcome problems or repeat successes takes time, so don't be concerned if you have trouble doing them at first. If you're a member of a writers' group, listen to your fellow writers and how they critique a piece. What suggestions or observations made sense, and why? Which ones seemed to come out of left field or were completely off the mark, and why? The author's verbal and non-verbal responses—and your own—to these suggestions will tell you a lot.

There's one last thing that makes this task tricky: the author is free to ignore your suggestions! Even if you think you're right, *right,* **right**, if the author thinks you're wrong, *wrong,* **wrong**, guess who wins? Not you. At least, not in the near term. Do your best, then tell your ego to go sit in the corner and be quiet. Everyone will be happier for it.

Reader Response: How Do You Feel?

The easiest thing a new critiquer can start with is how the piece made them feel. Readers will always have some kind of emotional response to a piece of writing. *Always.* "Emotional" doesn't mean extreme emotion: uncontrollable sobbing or rolling on the floor laughing. Boredom is also an emotional response. So are frustration, confusion, delight, even sexual arousal. "Emotional" covers the full range of reactions.

Did the work:

- Excite you?
- Anger you?
- Make you happy?
- Make you sad?
- Confuse you?
- Fascinate you?
- Annoy you?

- Thrill you?
- Bore you?
- Make you giggle?
- Make you swear?
- Make you stay up all night thinking about it? Or keep you thinking about it for days afterward?
- Make you throw it across the room?
- Make you want to bang your head against the wall?
- Something else entirely?
- All of the above?
- Some of the above?
- None of the above?

It could have done many of these things. Even a three-line haiku poem can do it.

Your first job as a critiquer is to capture how you reacted to the piece—and *why*, as best you can tell—so you can convey that to the author.

Driving Factors

Many factors drive or create your emotional response, but first and foremost is character behavior. Ask yourself how you are responding to these factors:

- How emotionally engaged are you with the characters? That is, how much or how little do you care about them and what's happening to them?
- What are the characters doing, thinking, saying, and feeling?
- How are they interacting with each other, their environment, and their situation?
- Are their behaviors consistent with or contrary to their situation or environment?
- Are their behaviors what you expected or assumed about them, or did they surprise you?

I'll go into these questions and many more in Book 4 (https://books2read.com/u/mYOzkM), which covers characterization in detail, plus point of view and dialogue.

Characters and Dialogue

Other things affect your emotional response, too. Setting comes to mind (think of the house in "The Fall of the House of Usher"), as do the story's structure, its tone and style, even its pace, but the primary driver will be the characters.

Authorial Intentions

Now you can ask more questions:

- *Why* did it make me feel that way?
- Is that what the author *wanted* me to feel?
- Why did the author want me to feel that way?

Now, of course, you can't have perfect knowledge of the author's intent if you're not the author (and sometimes not even when you are), but some elements of common sense apply. For example, if a scene seems like it's supposed to be sad but it's making you giggle, that's a problem. Or the scene is supposed to be funny and you're not getting even the slightest hint of a chuckle out of it.

However, a scene that's doing what it was meant to do—and doing it well—is, from a writer's (*and* reader's) perspective, a joy to read, even if it's making you bawl your eyes out or scream in fright. Especially then.

And of course, as I mentioned earlier, you can always ask the author what their intentions were.

Anticipation

Carly Simon once sang, "Anticipation is making me wait." And that's what writers want to do with readers: make them wait and keep them guessing about what's going to happen next.

In the context of critiquing, this is a two-edged sword. On the one hand, you want to be watching to see how well your fellow authors do that, including if they lead the reader astray *intentionally*.

On the other hand, *you* need to be careful about the assumptions you make, or at least be aware of them. If you assume a character is going to act a certain way or the plot is going to develop a certain way because that's what you *want* to happen, but then it doesn't, your critique will need to reflect what the author *did*, not what you wanted them to do—or note why what they did succeeded or failed.

Capture Your Response

Your next job as a reviewer is to capture for the author where they:

- Got it right—where the writing, the intent, and your response all came together
- Seemed to miss the target—where what the author apparently wanted you to feel isn't what you felt or left you confused or not knowing what to feel. Perhaps the intent was unclear, or the intention and the writing didn't quite match

Then, you need to identify *why* you responded that way. This requires that awareness—"right now I'm feeling [emotion] because [the characters are doing/saying/feeling/thinking *X*]"—and the ability to capture that awareness and write it down.

It can take some practice to develop the ability to ask and answer these questions as you read, but doing so will pay big dividends because everything else in this series will depend on you having that second train of thought running on a parallel track while you read.

Memory Skills

That bit of self-awareness means it's important for you to have a good but specialized memory. You can't let the words just flow in one eye and out the other, the way someone who's reading for pleasure can.

The words have to stop and make your acquaintance. Or, to put the focus in the right place, *you* have to make *theirs*.

It's very helpful if you can recall specific kinds of details—about what a character did or said before, for example, or how the author described something—even if it's been weeks or months since you last read a part of a work. (My group calls this "the chapter of the month club." I'll discuss it more later [*see page 15*]).

It takes a special kind of ability to hold details in your mind over a much longer period than an ordinary reader has to. That's not a skill everyone has. I believe some reviewers, perhaps most, who don't have it can develop it, but it takes conscious attention to the requirement, and a determination to learn how.

If you're a member of a critique group, you're potentially in an ideal place to learn how to do this. I say "potentially" because not all groups are created equal. For your group to be the right kind of learning environment, it helps to have at least one person who already has the working memory to track the kinds of details covered in this series, *and* can clearly and effectively communicate what they find, so you can learn from them.

Improving your memory for these details is an *active* process on your part. First, you have to read a work as closely as you can, *actively* trying to spot what worked and what didn't. This is the time to take plenty of notes, both on your overall response to the piece and on specific details. Those notes can help you spot trends in the writing too.

Second, it requires *actively* reading the critiques by and listening to the comments from the other reviewers during the meeting, or *actively* reading what other reviewers have posted online in order to learn from them. And, finally, *actively* rereading the piece, looking for what they found.

If you don't currently possess this kind of memory, it can be tempting to sit back and let the other people do the work. This is a mistake. It's also—to be blunt—lazy.

Learning how to do this really isn't any different from learning to read a text for its symbolism, theme, or deeper meaning—those things your high school English teacher tried to get you to write about in your term papers.

OK, maybe that's a bad memory. Sorry! But you remembered it. That's a start.

And this time, more than a mere letter grade is at stake.

The more you practice this skill, the better your powers of observation and your memory for these kinds of details will become. Trust me, you're not going to get it by osmosis. If it's not already a part of your skill set or you don't have that turn of mind, it's going to take effort to acquire it.

If you need some more motivation, keep this in mind: the better you learn how to critique someone else's work, the better you'll be able to evaluate and edit your own. And that means, when it's time for the group to review *your* work, they'll have a better work to review.

"The Chapter of the Month Club"

For long works, there's the extra challenge of "the chapter of the month club."[1] A twenty-chapter book could easily take a year to review if you look at a new chapter every two weeks. Earlier I discussed keeping track of details. Now expand that to keeping track of what went on in chapters you may have read a year ago, or more. Yeah, that can be hard.

---

[1] While every group operates differently, critiquing a draft of an entire book-length work, especially an early draft, is hard at best and often impractical. Limiting the number of pages the group will review at once can make it impossible to evaluate the story and character arcs within a chapter. For those reasons, my group has found that reviewing a submission a chapter at a time makes the most sense. We've found that if the chapter is very long—typically well above 20 pages—we'll allow ourselves extra time to ensure everyone has the time to give the piece the attention it deserves.

If your group distributes submissions electronically, in theory, you could go back to those earlier chapters to try to find what's bothering you. In theory.

In practice, that can be a time-consuming and frustrating process, even when using your word processor's "Find" function.

If you *can* hunt down that detail, great! But even just raising a question about something that doesn't seem quite right can be a big help. One of the beta readers for my third novel, *Wild Spread* (https://books2read.com/u/3LMeP7), asked how a character who'd gone blind earlier could now see other people's reactions. Thanks to his question, I fixed not only that scene but two earlier ones. The mistake he caught had slipped by everyone until he asked the question.

Wild Spread

Critiquing a long work one or two chapters at a time isn't ideal, but it's often the only practical way to review it. You just have to do the best you can.

No Rewriting!

Finally, when the writing isn't successful, try to suggest how the author might achieve what you think they meant to. *But do not rewrite the work for them*! Let me say that again.

Do not rewrite the work for the author!

Offer suggestions on how they might approach the change, but let—no, *make*—them do the work. They will grow only by doing the actual revising. And remember: it's *their* work, not yours.

So what's the difference between making suggestions and rewriting the work?

First, suggestions are tightly focused. For example, if you think the author could have chosen a better (clearer, more evocative, more descriptive) word or phrase, it's appropriate to suggest it and explain why. You might suggest they use "scurried" rather than "walked quickly" because it not only gets rid of the adverb, it tells the reader something about exactly *how* they walked. Or you might suggest "Porsche" rather than "sports car" if that's appropriate.

For anything much longer than a phrase or clause, though, it's better to state the problem and offer more general ways to overcome it: "This sentence confused me because... You could clarify it by...."

Second, be sure that a suggestion is clearly stated as a suggestion: "You might try... " or "How about...?" or "Consider...."

Rewriting, on the other hand, too often begins with some variant of "If I was writing this, I would... ." What this reviewer is saying is they want the author to write the piece to fit their (the reviewer's) style, preferences, etc. Sometimes the reviewer will skip that phrase, cross out the "offending" text, and insert their own. Either way, this disrespects the author and the work they've put into the piece. No matter how well-intentioned it is, it's just wrong. Don't do it.

Giving Praise

One of the real pleasures of being a critiquer, especially if you're part of a writers' group, is seeing new writers develop, watching their work get better and better with each revision or new chapter or story. When that happens, it's important to not only acknowledge those improvements but also to reinforce them by telling the writer what they did well and how it's better than their previous work.

What to Praise

A writer can succeed in many ways that deserve attention and praise, especially when they're things the author struggled with before. Here's just a partial list:

- A character description, whether a specific trait or the broader drawing of them.

- Dialogue that's crisp and clear—or intentionally vague as one character tries to deceive another, hides their true intentions, or doesn't know what they want.
- The description of a place, setting, or scene. This can range from a moment or a very localized place—a room—to an entire city, a swath of country side, or even a historical period.
- The description of an action, from a single, telling gesture, placed at just the right moment, all the way up to an entire scene, be it an act of caring—a love scene, say—or an act of violence—a murder, for example.
- The description of an emotion, particularly when it's done so your own emotions are engaged in an empathetic way: you *feel* what the character is feeling. This often happens through subtle descriptions of the character's behaviors as they experience those emotions, rather than through simplistic "telling." For example, in my book *The Eternity Plague* (https://books2read.com/u/3JMNzA), I show one of my character's emotions by having her run her fingertips back and forth along the edge of her desk. Between the dialogue surrounding this action and the action itself, it's clear Janet is uncertain about what she's supposed to do next.

    The Eternity Plague
- A particular word choice, turn of phrase, or passage that shines. A poet friend of mine once used the phrase "tincture of time" to describe the healing properties of allowing time to pass after a sad event. She captured the droplet-by-droplet pace of healing in the uncommon word tincture, then tied it into a nice bit of alliteration with the repeated t's and the hard-soft-soft-hard rhythm of the phrase.

I'll discuss these topics, and many more, in the other books in the series.

Of course, many other things might catch your attention and cause you to say "wow!" or "very nice!" or "that's *so* much better." Whatever the positive reaction, it's important to not just feel it yourself but to share that feeling with the author. Mark the phrase or passage in the manuscript and add a comment.

While a simple "Well done!" is nice, a more detailed comment is better, even if you're going to deliver the critique verbally as well. Using the example from my book above, a reviewer might have said, "I like the way you *showed* us Janet's uncertainty here rather than writing, 'Janet was uncertain.' Between her words and her gestures, we could tell she wasn't sure what she should do." Telling the writer why and how they succeeded helps them solidify their understanding so they'll be able to repeat it in the future.

Avoid Empty Praise

A few final words about praise. A vague, generic "Well, I liked it... " is ineffective because it doesn't tell the author anything they can build on. That's why throughout this series I will keep mentioning being specific. "Well, I liked it... " is too often a form of "social lubrication," an artificial way to try to maintain good relations or to make the author feel good about themself. Or it can be a sign that either the reviewer doesn't really know what to say or fears hurting the writer's feelings.

Praise should be given only when it's deserved.

While most writers, especially new ones, can use a boost to their self-esteem every now and then, that's *not* the purpose of critique. There's no place for empty fawning. No one should get a trophy and a parade down Main Street simply for submitting their work. Praise needs to be legitimately earned.

Bad Critique Techniques

Three unacceptable critique techniques need to be called out right now:

1. The ego-crusher. In this needlessly harsh technique, the critic does everything in their power to crush the soul of the writer. In my book on critique groups, *Finding the Write Fit* (https://

books2read.com/u/mYO8wY), I call groups that do this "The Destroyers" and "The Snobs." They might be blatant or subtle but the devastating effect is the same. You don't want to be a one-person version of either of those groups.

Finding the Write Fit

2. The fog. For fear of squashing the writer's fragile ego, the reviewer says nothing meaningful. Examples: "Oh, it was fine." Or, "Gee, I wouldn't... , you know...."
3. The liar. Related to #2, the reviewer lies rather than saying anything that might possibly be construed as being even the slightest bit critical: "It's perfect. Don't change a thing." Or worse, they fail to identify successes or failures because they want the author to produce work that's worse than the reviewer's. There's no place for this kind of jealousy in a critique group.

Critiquing a First Draft

Before I wrap up this chapter, I want to spend some time on first drafts, especially a first draft by a first-time author.

Should you critique a first draft, especially a new writer's first draft? There are three schools of thought on this, which I call the Yes School, the No School, and the It Depends School. I'll discuss these schools of thought in more detail in Book 2 (https://books2read.com/u/4NOogJ) but I can cover a few pieces of their philosophies here.

Actually, whether or not to critique a first draft is the wrong question. The better one is what should be critiqued and how.

Mechanics, Narrative, and Description

Let's start by taking a closer look at those two words: "first" and "draft." They both carry important meanings. "First": there will be more. "Draft": this is not a completed work, but a work in progress.

A first draft is the author's first encounter with the story. It's yours as the critiquer too, but the writer has to write it before you can read it. (I know, I know, I've got a firm grasp on the obvious.) But what that means is no matter how much advance work the author has done—writing character studies, laying out an outline, world-building, etc.—the story doesn't become a story until that first draft gets written. There's a lot the author doesn't know about their story, characters, and so on until they put all of them in the crucible together. Then *their* real learning starts, and that's where you have a role.

There's a lot *you* don't know about the story, too, so it's very important to not try to "fix" things. If the author is spending a lot of time—even whole chapters—on backstory or world-building, it's appropriate to call their attention to that and explain why it's not what the reader wants or needs, but then encourage them to keep going. It's also appropriate to discuss general techniques for how the author could weave nuggets of that material into the rest of the story, but emphasize that's a task for the next draft.

If there's a lot that needs fixing, you might want to focus on the things that need to be dealt with most urgently (that is, major problems with basics), or that can be addressed easily so the author can show some improvement right away. They probably can't fix everything right now—they don't know how yet—and overloading them with too many things to do may make them give up.

When it comes to mechanics—spelling, punctuation, and the rest—the Yes School thinks it's important to fix these errors before they become ingrained habits, if they aren't already, and undo them if they are. The No School thinks it's more important for the author to get that first draft written; there'll be plenty of time later to clean up these messes. And the It Depends School takes the position that critiquers need to evaluate both the problems and the author and make a decision based on what they see in both.

The vast majority of the first drafts you're going to come across, even by experienced authors, are going to be rough. Sometimes that's putting it mildly. An early draft by an experienced author will be rough in different ways than one by a new writer, but it will still have its problems. If you've already seen drafts like this, you know what I mean. If *you're* the new critiquer, expect this to be the case.

The fact that first drafts in particular can often be rough for hundreds of pages is still no excuse to be hard on the author, though. *They're first drafts.* If the writer's gotten that far into the piece, they've probably got the talent to string together a complete book. And for the first time in their life, they're trying to do it. Yes, they have a lot of work yet to do: drafts two and three and four and.... This is just the first one.

For shorter works, this is even truer. There will be *lots* of drafts.

But if you're too hard on a new author, especially regarding their very first submissions, maybe there won't be a draft two and a draft three and so on until it's done. Maybe they'll decide it isn't worth the continued abuse (their thought, not your intent!) to come to another meeting, much less go on to draft two and draft three and.... Or worse, they'll ignore everyone's inputs and self-publish something that isn't close to being ready.

Which would be an absolute shame.

Special Critique Tools

Critiquers today have some tools that deserve a quick mention. Word processing programs often have a macro functionality. A macro is a specialized program the user creates to perform a certain task that isn't already part of the software, or uses an existing capability in a unique way. I use macros to find and highlight certain words, phrases, or types of words, such as adverbs that end in -ly.

A former member of my writers' group had a thing about the word "that," which, to be honest, writers do overuse. So, if she had wanted to, she could have used the macro recorder in her word processor to have the find-and-replace function locate each instance of "that" in a piece and highlight it. This tool is valuable for calling an author's attention to words or phrases they're overusing (like "that"); dialogue tags other than said, asked, and thought; and so on.

And the great thing is, you don't need to know a whit about programming: the macro recorder follows along as you go through the steps you want the macro to do, and when you're done, it turns those steps into the programming code. Slick! More complex macros than one that looks for a single word do require some programming knowledge, but you can find plenty of help online. And, once the macro is created, you can use it again in other documents.

You can also run the text through a tool like ProWritingAid (https://prowritingaid.com/) or Grammarly (https://www.grammarly.com/) and recommend revisions based on those results. That presumes, of course, that the author hasn't already done it themself. If you want to use a technique like this, though, you'll need to have a paid account with that tool unless the piece is very short. These tools use artificial intelligence (AI) and machine learning (ML) more and more, so another alternative is to use an AI like the latest version of ChatGPT (https://chatgpt.com/overview) directly. Keep in mind, though, that as with ProWritingAid and Grammarly, you can only use limited features for free.

ProWritingAid

Grammarly

ChatGPT

Summing Up

This chapter has focused on the principles, practices, and tools of critiquing a work, and the other books in the series will go into them in much greater detail. But before we get to that, I need to talk about how you're going to deliver that critique to your fellow author and how to respond to the critiques you receive. That's what Chapter 2 is all about, and it begins on the next page.

Chapter 2

Delivering Your Critique

Life on the Other Side of the Critique

In addition to developing your own skills as a critiquer, you need to always be mindful of the person whose work you're reviewing. Remember, your job is to analyze their work, *not* to criticize *them*.

Think back to those bad critique techniques I mentioned earlier, and to my comments about first drafts. If you're going to deliver a critique in person, you'll get to see the author's initial reaction up close. If you're delivering it on an online critique site, it's even more important to remember the humanity of the person on the receiving side of the critique. The anonymity, or at least physical separation, of the internet is no excuse for being a jerk.

Or worse.

Think about how you'd feel—or have felt—when you got an unduly harsh or disrespectful critique.

As critiquers, we hold something very fragile in our hands—a new (or not so new) writer's ego, their hopes, their dreams—and if we only criticize without offering suggestions for ways to get better results, or if we fail to offer praise when it's deserved, we not only do no good, we may do harm.

That isn't to say we can't or shouldn't point out what isn't working or isn't working as well as it could. It's also not to say we need to sugarcoat everything, or be so namby-pamby or vague that what we say is as good as useless.

Writers do need to develop a thick skin. Once their work is published, they're going to get feedback, and those one- and two-star reviews can sting. The internet's trolls can be especially cruel.

But that does *not* mean we critiquers should be cruel.

It *does* mean we should always remember what it's like to be on the receiving end of a critique and do our work accordingly.

And that we should remember our critique is to help them, not overwhelm them. How much to critique a new writer on is a judgment call, but you don't have to shoot in the dark on it (to badly mix my metaphors). One technique that can help, especially with more-experienced authors, is to ask them what they most want the group to look for. Even so, it's impossible to know in advance if you "got it right" or not, so draw on whatever experience you have, what you're able to assess of the author's personality, make the call, and go with it.

Handling Overconfidence

New writers sometimes think they *know* how to write and their work needs, at most, minor tweaking. Then agents and editors will be falling all over themselves to offer six-figure advances, rush publication, a 50-city book tour with suites at the finest hotels, and so on. After all, their mother, or best friend, or whoever told them how great their work was!

Um... no.

OK, they *may* be the really rare writer who, like the Greek goddess Athena, bursts onto the scene fully formed with a quiver full of literary arrows and the knowledge on how to use them.

Your newbie is that one-in-a-gazillion author, right? Right?

Would that it were so.

More likely, the piece is going to need work. Maybe a lot of work.

None other than Ernest Hemingway supposedly said, "All first drafts are shit."

The draft in front of you probably won't be quite that bad. But how do you tell that new, overconfident writer without shattering their confidence, self-image, will to live, and so on that their work needs improving?

The answer for this kind of writer is not that different from how you critique a more-experienced writer's work. You tell them, honestly but gently, firmly, and with clear specifics what needs work and how they can make the piece better—without rewriting it for them.

That's what the rest of this series is about. You'd think I planned it that way.

Handling Lack of Confidence

On the other end of the confidence spectrum—and it *is* a spectrum that authors travel back and forth on all the time—is lack of confidence. *Every* author experiences it at some time. Even the most experienced writers suffer from some degree of it every day. The kind that afflicts these authors is called "impostor syndrome," where the writer feels—even if they've been on the *New York Times* bestseller list repeatedly—they truly have no skills, they're a complete fraud, and that's going to be revealed for all to see any day now.

It's not true, but that's how they feel.

For the new writer, especially when they encounter more-experienced writers for the first time, or get their first critique back, it's easy to fall into this trap. And if they were unsure of their abilities to start with, it's even easier.

That first submission to a critique group, whether it's a new author's first-ever submission or a writer's first submission to a new-to-them group, is always a nervous time. It takes courage to put your work in front of a bunch of strangers, especially a group you know is going to look for its weaknesses (*and* strengths, but the new writer may have no idea what they are or if there are any) and point them out.

This is where it's vital—absolutely vital—for the reviewer to highlight anything the author did well and to be encouraging and helpful in the rest of their critique. However, this does *not* mean giving praise for the sake of giving praise, as I pointed out earlier *(see page 16)*. The plaudits still need to be earned.

It's also helpful to remind the new writer that *every* big-name writer, and every member of the group, was once a newbie too. Every career starts somewhere, and that somewhere is the beginning. (Another blinding grasp of the obvious, but sometimes it needs to be said.)

For the member who's been part of the group for a while and has hit one of those confidence potholes—which sometimes seem as deep and wide as the Grand Canyon—you should not only give justified praise for the good elements of a piece but also remind them of the quality of their former work and the group's belief in the writer's abilities.

Maybe it's just this one submission that hasn't lived up to their standards. Or maybe it's an on-going funk. Whatever it might be, sometimes critiquers have to take the role of a support group to hold their member's spirits up until they find their groove again.

Defending, Explaining, and Arguing

A new author may want to argue with you, defend or explain their work, etc. Don't let them.

For starters, the work does *not* need defending. Fixing, probably. Defending, no.

Any author is likely to have a defensive first response, even if the comments aren't negative. That's natural. Any suggestion to do things a different way is going to get that. Becky Levine wrote a blog post titled "Critique Comments: Remembering to Give Them Time" (https://tinyurl.com/2htm6yst). She advised letting a

Critique Comments: Remembering to Give Them Time

critique you receive sit and percolate or ferment (my words, her concept) before responding to it. That defensive reaction needs to be put aside, taken off the hot stove, and allowed to cool, as it were.

It might be wrong.

Or it might not.

But in the heat of that first reactive moment, it can be hard to tell. Be sure to help the author understand this.

That happened with *this* chapter. One of the reviewers of the first draft asked if a section needed to be where it was or if it belonged somewhere else. My first reaction was this was the right place, dadgummit, but after thinking about it some more, I decided she was right and moved it.

Of course, the author may want to defend the choices they made because those choices set up things that will happen later. That *is* something to keep in mind. You know less about the future direction of the story than the author does, especially if they've laid out a story outline. Accept that defense provisionally and wait to see if what the author says they've planned actually happens.

> **Note: there are no spoilers in a critique group, and this is exactly the situation where that applies.**

You *can* point out that if the work, or a part of it, needs to be explained, that's a sign it isn't complete. After all, the author isn't going to be able to sit next to each future reader and explain what the text or passage was supposed to mean when they stumble over something. All the reader has to go by is what's on the page. If it's not clear, even if only one or two members of the group have trouble with it, it needs to be looked at. If three or more do, there should be no doubt some kind of fix is in order. Yes, readers *can* be willing to wait for an explanation but that willingness often depends on whether they have even a slight sense the confusing item is there for a reason. If something is just confusing, especially if this is not the first time they've stumbled, their patience is going to wear thin.

Arguing is also not acceptable behavior. It's a sign the author isn't ready to learn, and learning how to be a better writer *should* be why they're a member of a critique group. It's hard to swallow your initial response, say "Thank you for your suggestion," and move on. (Been there. More times than I can count.) But it's necessary.

You can head off this kind of behavior in a few ways. First, right from the get-go, let each new member know how the group operates and what its expectations are. My group actually has an "expectations" document we give to prospective members after they make initial contact with us. I've included a copy in Appendix 2 (page 53). If you want to use it as a model, you can download a copy here (https://thecritiquedoctor.com/resources/).

The Critique Doctor

Second, set a good example. Whatever you say your "rules" are for the group, live by them. My group does this by scheduling the review of a prospective member's first submission after all other work for that meeting. That way the newbie will be able to experience how we work before we turn our attention to them.

And then, enforce the rules with the new member. When they try to argue, defend, or explain, gently but firmly remind them that's not the way you work, and why. It may take more than just the group's leader to get that message across if the "gently but firmly" method doesn't work at first. But do it. If the newbie doesn't want to hear what you have to say and doesn't come back, it's their loss, not yours.

If they understand you care about them as a writer and want them to succeed, while they may go home with their tail between their legs—we've *all* done that at some point, right?—they'll be back next time, and their work will get better.

And *that*, my friends, is one of the best rewards for giving great critique.

Different Learning Styles

There's one other thing to think about. Different people learn and absorb information differently. Some do best by reading new information. Others need to see it demonstrated. Still others need to hear it. And yet others learn best by doing a particular task. In-person and online critique group reviews tend to be written, with an oral summary or discussion at the group meeting. Critiques on a website are almost always written. In fact, I haven't found an online critique site that accepts or allows critiques any other way.

But what happens if your way of providing critique doesn't connect with the way the author learns best? I currently have a critique group member who does a lot better if he not only hears the individual comments, but has a chance to practice making the corrections. Written comments and guides don't exactly go in one eye and out the other, but they don't stick as well as they would for someone else. One-on-one, step-by-step reviews with him doing the editing in real time takes time, but if the time spent makes a big difference in the areas he's having trouble with, it's worth it. However, this sort of work needs to be done outside of the group's regular meetings.

Planning How You'll Deliver Your Critique

Each article in the other books in the series will address discussing your findings, whether good or problematic, with the author of the work, but always in the context of the topic of that particular article. While those findings, and your suggestions on how to address or improve on them, are the components of a complete critique, they aren't the whole thing. You also need to think about your observations in the context of the entire piece. Taken together, the whole will be greater than the sum of its parts.

How you organize your findings and recommendations depends to some degree on the author and the work. A more-experienced or capable writer will probably not need the same level of detail as a less experienced one, and you'll likely discuss different topics. Also, too much detail can overwhelm a new writer.

In Chapter 1, I discussed the three schools of thought *(see page 19)* around whether or not to critique a first draft: Yes, No, and It Depends. If you're a member of the Yes or It Depends Schools, you may find it most helpful to your author to focus on just one or a few things in a particular critique, while leaving other problem areas for later drafts or chapters. I've even gone so far as to do some intensive, one-on-one tutoring outside of group time with writers who were having serious trouble overcoming specific problems. This approach isn't for everyone, but it may do the most good if you have the knowledge, temperament, and time to do it.

With face-to-face groups, you need to consider how much time you have available. Some groups set—and enforce—very strict time limits for each reviewer. If you have only three to five minutes to speak, your choices of what to say and what to leave in your written comments are going to be a lot different than if there's no time limit.

Another consideration is whether you deliver the critique verbally, in writing, or both. I've never encountered a group that only provided verbal critiques, but online sites are almost always limited to written comments. Most in-person groups do both: each reviewer will discuss certain topics but will also make comments, corrections, or suggestions in or on the text and/or in a separate document.

Even though these considerations will be part of the standard practice of the group, you may find you'll use them to guide and shape what you say and how you say it if you're critiquing a work on a site.

My group has developed a set of critique guides: one for fiction and memoir *(see page 41)*, one for creative nonfiction *(see page 45)*, one for "straight" or functional nonfiction *(see page 49)*, and one for poetry *(see page 51)*. We've found over the years that these types of writing are different enough—functional nonfiction tends not to use dialogue, for example—that we needed separate guides for each. They're included in Appendix 1 *(see page 41)* and you can download them from my website (https://thecritiquedoctor.com/resources/). These guides each list a dozen or so broad topics we use to shape our critiques and discussions—everything I'll cover in Books 2 through 5, in fact. We generally don't discuss our comments in the text unless we're using them to point out specific examples.

The Critique Doctor

Delivering the Critique

One important consideration is where—that is, in what forum—you'll present your critique. If you're part of a group that meets face-to-face, whether that's with everyone in the same physical room, virtually, or in a hybrid setting, the dynamic is different from posting a review on a critique site, where there's rarely any direct personal interaction.

In Person

Delivering a critique in person has both advantages and risks. The most obvious advantage is that you and the author can discuss your suggestions in real time. You can monitor the author's responses and tell how well or poorly they're taking your suggestions. But that takes us right into the areas of risk, doesn't it?

Knowing your target audience is as important to you as it is to the author.

- What help and advice do they need most?
- How much can they absorb?
- How well have they accepted and implemented your suggestions in the past?
- What would be most useful to them at this moment in their writer's journey?

These are judgments you'll have to make before you present every critique. If your delivery is more aggressive or critical than it needs to be *in the author's eyes*, that can lead to arguments or worse.

At the same time, as I've noted elsewhere in the book, the author must understand they don't need to defend themself or their work. They shouldn't feel that they or it are under attack, and indeed, they should *not* be under attack.

Also, the author shouldn't have to explain a lot of things about the work.

> **Note: spoilers are not a consideration in a critique group. However, it is fair for them to let the group know if a particular element is a setup for something that will happen later—but then they should reveal what that something is.**

This kind of explanation may put your review in a new light, maybe even completely invalidate it. That's OK: you and the author will both learn something from the conversation.

That said, it's appropriate to remind the author they're not going to be able to sit next to each reader and explain what they meant whenever the reader gets confused.

In Writing for In-Person Delivery

You can deliver your written critique in two ways: on a separate sheet or form or in the document itself. Nothing says you can't do both. In fact, that's how my group operates. We write comments in our guides and put comments in the text too. These comments can be handwritten or inserted using your word processor's tools.

Handwritten Comments

Legibility is the key factor in handwritten comments: just because *you* can read your handwriting doesn't mean someone else can! How large or small your handwriting is can make a difference too. My handwriting tends to be fairly small, which lets me squeeze a lot of words into a small space, but I get occasional complaints about that. On the other hand, if your handwriting is naturally large, it may be hard to fit many comments, or comments with any depth, onto a work, even if the text is double-spaced, as it should be. Writing sideways in the margins works, but if you're distributing your reviews electronically, people may have trouble reading your sideways-oriented notes in the scanned copy.

Use the standard set of editor's marks to identify recommended insertions, deletions, upper or lower cases, and the like. The NY Book Editors website has one of the better examples (https://tinyurl.com/553942ey) I've seen. It not only shows the marks, it demonstrates how they're used.

NY Book Editors

Computer-Inserted Comments

If you use your word processor's tools to insert your comments into the manuscript, you have a couple of options: inline or via a reviewing or commenting function.

Inline commenting means placing your observations or recommended changes directly in the text. If you choose to do this, be sure to make your comments and suggestions easy to spot by highlighting them, **boldfacing them**, putting them in a different color, **a distinctly different font**, or some combination of these. If you want to recommend deleting a word, a phrase, or even an entire paragraph, many word processors have a strike-through function which draws a line right through the material you want to suggest be deleted, ~~like this~~.

The main disadvantage to making inline comments is, over the course of the piece, they'll change where the page breaks occur. This isn't a huge problem, and it's likely to happen anyway if you and the author use different word processors, but it does make finding a particular comment a bit more difficult if you want to discuss it with the author.

The other way to make comments or suggestions right in the text is with your word processor's Track Changes function in its Review or Comment tool. (Other programs may use different names for their equivalent tools.) Track Changes lets you make changes to the text (spelling corrections, insertions, deletions, etc.) and identifies them through color coding, various kinds of underlines, and other techniques. The author can accept or reject the suggestions and the software will make the accepted changes right away.

The commenting function allows you to select the material you want to comment on and type your thoughts into a comment box, sometimes called a balloon, that will appear in an expanded right margin. (The size of the text in the body of the manuscript shrinks to make room in the margin, but it also keeps the pagination—where the page breaks occur—the same as the original.) If you use the Review function in conjunction with Track Changes, you can explain why you're suggesting a change, if that's appropriate.

The weakness of providing critique comments in the text is they will focus on very specific things but fail to address the bigger picture of the piece. That's why critique guides, like the ones my group developed, are so valuable: they get critiquers' noses out of the text and demand they think more broadly about the work and bigger topics.

In Writing on an Online Site

Delivering critiques on an online site has its own challenges. These sites may:

- Have their own form for comments
- Require you to post your comments in the discussion thread that includes the piece you're reviewing
- Require you to insert inline comments
- Give you the option to use one or several of these options

With an in-person critique, you can immediately clear up any misunderstandings, but when you're delivering a written review on a critique site, the reader could misinterpret what you wrote and that can be hard to correct.

Plus, you can easily forget that the author of the work you've reviewed is a real person, causing you to be harsher than necessary. The distinction between an honest critique and a brutally honest one, with emphasis on "brutally," can sometimes be very fine. And that perception is entirely in the eye of the person receiving the critique or others who read it.

Also, it's possible for the reviewer to understand what they meant but for the author to not understand. This is less of a potential problem if the site allows or requires comments to be placed within the text, but if the comments are posted after the end of the piece or on a separate form, vague, indirect references to places in the text can lead to confusion.

Whenever you post a critique on one of these sites, it's smart to step back from the comments, maybe even hold them for a day if you can, and review them with fresh eyes before you click the "Post" or "Publish" button.

Clear and Specific, but...

As I've said throughout the book, and will repeat in the rest of the series, no matter how you deliver your critique comments, they should be as clear and specific as you can make them. Suggestions about alternatives can be very helpful because you might see connections (or disconnects) the author did not or might simply find a different way of saying something that communicates more effectively.

There's a very important caveat here, however. Always, always, always keep in mind that it is *not* your job to rewrite the piece for the author. Let me say that again.

It is not your job to rewrite the piece for the author.

Banish the phrases "if I was writing this" or "if this was my [story, article, poem, etc.]" from your critique vocabulary. You're *not* writing the work; the author is. If you want to suggest alternative ways to write something, use terms like "you might consider" or "try this instead," and then explain why you think the alternative is better.

But remember, the author has the absolute right to decide not to follow your suggestions.

It's *their* story. Period.

Delivery Techniques

Mark Twain supposedly defined tact as "the art of telling a man to go to Hell in such a way as to make him eager to begin the journey." Your critiques will be best if they mix honesty with tact.

So how do you deliver a critique effectively? Here are a couple of techniques you can use regardless of where or how you're delivering your critique.

Soft-Hard-Soft

In this technique, the reviewer begins their remarks with something they liked about the piece—and why—goes on to the things that need improvement, and then closes with another positive element. While few works will be so completely awful there are *no* good things in them, reviewers shouldn't twist themselves into pretzels trying to come up with something good to say. They should also avoid saying only positive things. Gushing, or worse, faint praise, is as bad as nuclear annihilation of a piece.

General-to-Specific

This technique can be applied with the first. This is where the review guides in Appendix 1 *(see page 41)*, or something like them, can come in handy. If the author's characterizations were not what they could have been, a reviewer can start with an overall discussion of characterization techniques and then focus on how the author could have done better in particular instances. But they should be careful not to get too far down into the weeds. They can offer ideas and suggestions—I'll provide some ways to do this in later books in the series—but it's *not* their job to rewrite the story for the author. I can't emphasize this point enough!

Final Authority

In the end, remember that no matter what changes you suggest, the author has the absolute power to ignore them. Maybe, in their eyes, they were wholly inappropriate. Maybe they didn't fit with how they intended the story to develop, or the character to behave, or something else. Maybe the suggestions were premature, ones that might be appropriate in a later draft. Maybe they don't understand them.

Whatever the reason, it's the author's call. It's also their right to change their mind later. In any case, don't take their decision to not accept your suggestion personally. After all, you have that same right when your work is under review.

Time to Get to Work

If you've decided to be a member of a critique group or join an online critique site, you've taken on an important responsibility and obligation. Other writers are trusting you to give them the best feedback and advice you can. They're seeking not only to improve the specific piece they've put in front of you—and taking the risk to their ego doing so involves—they're seeking to improve their knowledge of the craft of writing and how they turn that knowledge into words on the page. Book learning is fine and necessary, but writing, like any other craft or art form, is about the doing, the creation of the images, ideas, people, emotions, and events that combine to tell an engaging story, one the reader doesn't want to—make that *can't*—put down.

And the fact that you've joined the group or site, or are independently reviewing a work for another writer, indicates you also want to improve your own craft. If you take the task of critiquing seriously, you can't help but do so. When critique is done well, both the reviewer and the author benefit.

So how can you do that, and do it well? That's what the rest of this series is all about. The next three books cover everything from the mechanics of spelling, punctuation, grammar, and so on, to narrative, dialogue, setting, characterization, all the way up to theme and plot.

The last book will give you, if you're a prose writer, the insights and tools you'll need to critique poetry effectively.

Critiquing is an act of "paying it forward," of giving in order to receive. That's the social contract of any critique group or site. It's a demanding contract, and one not everyone is willing to sign, but if you have, on behalf of your fellow authors, I thank you.

Appendices

Use these appendices to help you create and provide a critique and give guidance to new members.

Appendix 1 *(see page 41)* contains the latest versions of the fiction and memoir, nonfiction, and poetry critique guides the Cochise Writers' Group uses. Be sure to check the website (https://thecritiquedoctor.com/) for the most current versions or to download copies for your group's use.

Appendix 2 *(see page 53)* contains the latest version of the Cochise Writers' Group's expectations document, which describes how the group operates and what we expect from our members. Be sure to check the website (https://thecritiquedoctor.com/) for the most up-to-date version or to download a copy for your group's use, with appropriate modifications.

The Critique Doctor

Appendix 1

Critique Guides

Critique groups can use the following guides to "raise their focus" from individual, line-by-line errors and successes to the broader aspects of the craft of telling a story. Use the layouts below to create your own guide documents, or download the current versions as Microsoft Word forms from my website (https://thecritiquedoctor.com/resources). Other formats may be available in the future. If you choose to use the layouts below or the downloaded forms, please remember they are protected by copyright. You may use them for critiques within your group but may not share them outside of the group.

The Critique Doctor

FICTION AND MEMOIR CRITIQUE GUIDE

Critique of:

By:

From:

GENRE (Is this work a memoir or a fictional piece? If fiction, what is its genre [science fiction, romance, mystery, etc.]? Many fiction genres are further broken down into narrower categories called subgenres. Science fiction includes subgenres like space opera, post-apocalyptic, and steampunk. Romance includes subgenres like steamy, sweet, and historical. If you can tell, what is this work's subgenre?)

OPENING (Does the opening quickly grab the reader's attention and interest? Does it seem to begin *in medias res*, that is, in the middle of the action, or does it spend too much time on backstory and world-building? Is the scene, chapter, story, or book protagonist introduced right away? Is the problem they're facing introduced right away?)

CONFLICT & TENSION (Is there conflict between characters? Note: "conflict" does not necessarily mean violence; it may be physical, emotional, psychological, or a combination of these; it may be direct or indirect. Is there tension within, between, and among the characters in the piece? Does the tension ebb and flow within the piece, while increasing overall from beginning to end? Does the reader experience this tension?)

STAKES (Are the stakes—that is, what's at risk and the consequences of that risk—to the characters, especially the protagonist and antagonist clear? Are they significant enough in the context of the piece to maintain the reader's interest?)

STORY ARC, PLOT, AND SUBPLOTS (Story arc: Do the conflict and tension of the piece overall and each of its components—scene and chapter, if appropriate—increase to a climax and resolution over the course of the piece? Plot: Do the main events of the piece move it forward along its arc? Subplots: Are there sequences of events that are subsidiary to the main plot but affect it in some way? Is it clear how these sets of events affect the main plot? [They may not be at the scene or chapter level.])

DESCRIPTION & SETTING (Does the author provide sufficient detail for the reader to develop a clear picture of the time, place, and situation of the piece? Is there so much information that it interferes with the flow of the story? Is important information missing?)

SHOW VS. TELL (Does the author use both techniques—"showing" through the use of sensory details, or presenting the actions or thoughts of characters to illustrate their emotional state, for example, and "telling" through narrative reporting? Is the balance of "showing" versus "telling" appropriate for the piece?)

POINT OF VIEW (Does the author maintain a consistent point of view—that is, which character's senses does the reader experience the story through—or does it wander? If the POV is not consistent, did the author signal very early in the piece they were going to do this as a creative choice?)

CHARACTERIZATION (Are the characters believable? Are they "three dimensional," that is, are enough aspects of their personalities presented that they become human [or understandable, if not human] to the reader? Note: characters do not have to be likable. Are the motivations for their actions clear, or do they become clear over time?)

DIALOGUE (Do the conversations between the characters "sound natural" to the reader? Do the words chosen, their order, and the use of emphasis communicate their emotions? Do the characters use dialogue to deliver information to each other and/or to the reader in "info-dumps?" Is any use of dialect or jargon limited to only what is necessary to establish certain characteristics of the speaker?)

NARRATIVE VOICE OR STYLE (Is the style of the writing consistent throughout the piece and appropriate to the story? Does the way the author tells the story contribute to its mood at each point?)

PACING (Does the speed at which the story seems to pass fit with the events, mood, and degree of conflict and tension of the moment? Does it maintain the reader's interest or allow it to wander?)

STRUCTURE & FLOW (Does the sequence in which the events of the plot are presented allow the reader to understand and maintain their interest in the story? Do events move naturally from one to the next? If they do not, is this intentional on the part of the author, for example, to illustrate conflict or increase tension?)

CLOSING (Does the ending of a book or story provide a satisfying conclusion, that is, one in which all of the major story questions have been resolved? If the closing is to a scene, chapter, or longer work that is not the last in a series, does it leave some things unresolved to pique the reader's curiosity and encourage them to continue reading?)

MECHANICS (Are there any problems with the format of the text, grammar, spelling, punctuation, capitalization, etc.? Are any places unclear or confusing? If so, what caused this and how can they be improved?)

OTHER (Use this space to address any other problems or successes that were not covered in any of the other categories.)

OVERALL IMPRESSION (What is your overall impression of the piece? Does it "work," that is, is it effective at telling its story? Why or why not? Were you confused in places where that didn't seem to be the author's intent? Is something about the piece especially successful?)

CREATIVE NONFICTION CRITIQUE GUIDE

Critique of:

By:

From:

Creative nonfiction is different from "straight" or "functional" nonfiction. The former includes biographies and autobiographies (but *not* memoirs), personal essays, travelogues, editorials or opinion pieces, etc. Any piece, in other words, that tells a story—and so employs many of the techniques of fiction—while being centered in facts. Straight nonfiction, on the other hand, is strictly factual, for example, reports, how-to guides, or studies.

Because of the variety of work that comprises creative nonfiction, some of the criteria below will not apply to all pieces. These are identified with asterisks (*). Skip them if they do not apply. Be sure to also identify things the author did particularly well and why they were so effective.

TITLE (If present. Does the title give a clear indication of what the piece is about? Does it draw the reader's interest?)

GENRE OR TYPE (What kind of piece is this? For example, is it a personal essay, a biography, an article for a newsletter or a blog, or a devotional?)

TARGET AUDIENCE OR MARKET (Who are the piece's intended readers? Is it appropriate for them? Is the piece intended to be part of a book, such as a collection of essays, or is it meant to stand alone? If it's to stand alone, does it fit well in the market the author selected? If you know, how well does it fit that market? What other markets might the author consider?)

OPENING (Does the opening quickly grab your attention and interest? Does it immediately identify the piece's topic or purpose and, if appropriate, the people involved, the lessons the author wants to share, etc.? Does it establish the author's voice and authority, if appropriate? If the piece is the second or later one in a connected series, does it establish that connection?)

* CONFLICT & TENSION (Some kinds of works, like an investigative report or a history, involve conflict between people. If this is the case, does the piece make that conflict and the reasons for it clear? Does it convey the tensions that existed among the participants and create tension in you as the conflict grows?)

* STAKES (Does the piece identify which of the characters had something to gain or lose, and how significant it was to them and to others? Does it make clear what the consequences of gaining or losing that were for everyone involved? It's possible a final resolution has not been achieved yet or may not be achievable at all. In that case, does it identify what that means for all concerned?)

* STORY ARC, PLOT, AND SUBPLOTS (Subplots will likely not be relevant [or even possible] if the piece is short. However, any piece that tells a story should identify an initial problem, contain increasing action or conflict, a climax, and some kind of resolution, perhaps an incomplete one. Those events define the arc and plot. Are they present? Are they effectively related?)

* DESCRIPTION & SETTING (Does the author provide sufficient detail for you to develop a clear picture of the time, place, and situation of the piece? Is there so much information that it interferes with the flow of the story? Is important information missing? If so, what?)

SHOW VS. TELL (Does the author use both techniques: "showing" through, for example, the use of sensory details, or presenting the actions of characters to illustrate their emotional state; and "telling" through narrative reporting? Is the balance of "showing" versus "telling" appropriate for the piece?)

POINT OF VIEW or VIEWPOINT (This kind of work can use "point of view" [POV] in the fiction sense or "viewpoint" in the nonfiction sense, or both. In the former case—for biographies, histories, and personal essays, for example—do you experience the story consistently through the perspective of one character? Or, if the piece contains multiple POV characters, are those POVs clearly distinguished and separated? For other pieces, does the author clearly express their opinion or perspective? Do they give appropriate attention to other viewpoints or approaches? Do they "prove" their viewpoint with data and evidence, or are they offering opinions or hearsay as fact?)

CHARACTERIZATION (Every piece will have at least one character, if only the author. Does the author clearly identify the central character—the protagonist—early on? Does the author identify opposing characters—the antagonist(s)—and the reason for their opposition to the protagonist? Does the author provide enough information about each character to "bring them alive?" Do they seem like real people? Does the author provide information about each character's personality, motivations, interests, fears, or concerns, as appropriate and necessary, as opposed to simply describing their appearance?)

* DIALOGUE (If there is more than one character in the piece, and they talk to each other, do their conversations feel natural to your mental ear? Try reading them out loud. Do they sound natural? Do the characters use dialogue to deliver information to each other and/or to the reader in "info-dumps?" Is any use of dialect or jargon limited to only what is necessary to establish certain characteristics of the speaker? NOTE: "Dialogue" includes interior monologue, or thought—the character talking to themself. This too should sound like a real person speaking, even if they're not speaking out loud.)

NARRATIVE VOICE OR STYLE (Is the style of the writing consistent throughout the piece and appropriate to the story and its genre? Does the way the author tells the story contribute to its mood at each point?)

PACING (Does the speed at which the story passes fit with the events, mood, and degree of conflict and tension of the moment? Does it maintain your interest or does it allow your mind to wander?)

STRUCTURE & FLOW (Does the sequence of the events of the piece, or the observations or assertions and arguments, allow you to understand and maintain your interest in the piece? Do the events, observations, or assertions and arguments move naturally from one to the next? If they do not, is this intentional on the part of the author, for example, to illustrate conflict or increase tension?)

CLOSING (Does the end of the piece provide a satisfying conclusion—that is, one in which all of the major story questions have been resolved—if appropriate? Or, do the observations, assertions, or arguments lead to a logical conclusion, even if you do not agree with it? If the closing is to a scene, chapter, or longer work that is not the last in a series, does it leave some things unresolved to pique your curiosity and encourage you to continue reading?)

MECHANICS (Are there any problems with grammar, spelling, punctuation, capitalization, the format of the text, etc.? Are there any places that are unclear or confusing? If there are, what made them so and how can they be improved?)

OTHER (Use this space to discuss any other problems or successes that were not addressed in the other categories.)

OVERALL IMPRESSION (What is your overall impression of the piece? Does it "work," that is, is it effective at telling its story? Why or why not? Were you confused in places where that didn't seem to be the author's intent? Is something about the piece especially successful?)

NONFICTION CRITIQUE GUIDE

Critique of:

By:

From:

"Straight" or "functional" nonfiction is different from creative nonfiction. The former is strictly factual, for example, reports, how-to guides, or studies. Creative nonfiction, on the other hand, includes biographies, autobiographies (but *not* memoirs), personal essays, travelogues, editorials/opinion pieces, etc. Any piece, in other words, that tells a story—and so employs many of the techniques of fiction—while being centered in facts.

Because of the variety of work that comprises straight nonfiction, some of the criteria below will not apply to all pieces. Skip them if they do not apply. Be sure to also identify things the author did particularly well and why they were so effective.

TITLE (If present, does the title give a clear indication of what the piece is about? Does it draw the reader's interest?)

OPENING (Does the opening give a clear sense of what the piece is going to be about? Does it motivate the reader to continue?)

TOPIC & MAIN POINTS (Is it clear what the topic of the piece is? Are the main points identifiable and clearly expressed?)

SHOW VS. TELL (Did the author use clear and relevant examples to illustrate, demonstrate, or clarify their points?)

VIEWPOINT (If appropriate, is the author advocating or supporting a particular position? If so, do they do it clearly? Do they give appropriate attention to other viewpoints or approaches? Do they "prove" their viewpoint with data and evidence, or are they offering opinions or hearsay as fact?)

STRUCTURE & FLOW (Does the piece move from point to point in an orderly and logical sequence? Are there clear connections between the points, and clear transitions from one to the next?)

DEPTH & COMPLETENESS (Does the piece seem to cover the subject matter in sufficient depth, or is the reader left with unanswered questions? Conversely, does the author go into more detail than is necessary?)

NARRATIVE VOICE OR STYLE (Are these appropriate for the subject matter and target audience, if known? Do they make the information presented easier or harder to absorb?)

PACING (Does the pace help hold the reader's attention, or does it provide opportunities for the reader's mind to wander? Conversely, does the pace move too quickly? For example, are important points underemphasized or not given enough weight?)

CLOSING (Does the closing wrap up the piece effectively? Does it provide a summary, for example, that helps solidify the material in the reader's mind? If the piece is part of a larger work, does it make the reader want to continue to the next portion?)

MECHANICS (Are there any problems with grammar, spelling, punctuation, capitalization, etc.? Keep in mind that text formatting techniques such as section headings, sidebars, pull quotes, illustrations, etc., may not be appropriate for an early draft. They will be developed later as the work matures.)

OTHER (Use this space to address any other problems or successes that were not covered in any of the other categories.)

OVERALL IMPRESSION (What is your overall impression of the piece? Does it "work," that is, is it effective at relating its information? Why or why not? Were you confused in places where that didn't seem to be the author's intent? Is something about the piece especially successful?)

POETRY CRITIQUE GUIDE

Critique of:

By:

From:

EMOTIONAL RESPONSE (Did the poem make you feel something? If so, what? What was its mood or tone? Did it give you a particular insight into something, or leave you still thinking about it after you'd put it down?)

TITLE (If present, does the title give a clear indication of what the poem is about or set the scene? Does it draw your interest? Is it the first or last line of the poem?)

IMAGERY (Does the poem create an image in your mind? Remember, this can involve any of the senses, plus emotions. How many senses does the poet use? Are the images specific and concrete? Does a particular image stand out or do any need to be stronger?)

SOUND (When read out loud, do you hear any rhyming words—either at the ends of lines or within lines—or other kinds of repeated sounds? Does the poet use words that sound like the things they represent? Do any of these feel natural and contribute to the flow and effect of the poem, or do they feel forced or awkward?)

RHYTHM & FLOW (When read aloud, does the poem have a flow to it that lets you read it smoothly? Does it consistently move in the same direction? If lines were written to follow particular patterns of stressed and unstressed syllables, does the poet follow those patterns consistently, or do they break the pattern at times? If the latter, does that seem to be intentional?)

LANGUAGE (Does the poet use creative and evocative turns of phrase, or do they use clichés? Do they make comparisons in interesting ways, or ordinary ones? Are the words at the beginning and end of each line strong? Do they resonate? Does the poem have a compelling ending? If rhyme was used, is it natural and unforced? If repetition is used, does it emphasize or distract?)

FORM & LAYOUT (If the poem is written in a particular poetic form—e.g., limerick, haiku, sonnet, etc.—does it follow the line count, line length, stress pattern, and other requirements of the form? If not, where does it not comply? Is anything about how the poem appeared on the page particularly effective or interesting? Does that shape connect with the subject?)

MECHANICS (Does it contain problems with verb tenses, noun/verb disagreements, point of view shifts, etc.? Are the verbs active or passive? Does the punctuation help clarify the poem, or does it add confusion? [Remember, punctuation in a poem can be quite different from that in prose.])

WAS ANYTHING MISSING (Do you feel something is needed to make it more effective at what it was meant to do?)

COULD ANYTHING HAVE BEEN DELETED (Could the poem be more effective if any parts are removed? Does it contain descriptions or images that don't contribute or seem excessive? Is there anything else that doesn't seem to contribute to the poem, reducing its effectiveness?)

OTHER/OVERALL (What is your overall response to the poem? Put any observations that don't fit in the other categories here.)

Appendix 2

Cochise Writers' Group Expectations Document

An expectations document sets the ground rules for a new member and defines how the group operates. Give it to a prospective member even before they join the group. Doing so can either help them gain confidence that this group will work for them, or help them decide the group is going to expect more of them than they can or are willing to give. Expectations should be specific and laid out clearly but also allow for flexibility when life intrudes or a writer isn't producing work they want the group to review.

Feel free to use the text below as a model. Add to or subtract from it as the needs and capabilities of your group require.

**Cochise Writers' Group:
What We Do and What We Expect From Our Members**

The Cochise Writers' Group is a professional organization. By "professional," we mean we are committed to doing the work needed to improve our own writing and to helping the other members of the group improve theirs. It does not mean we are necessarily making money from our writing—yet. This paper lays out how we run our meetings and what we expect of our members.

Meetings and Participation

- Meetings begin promptly at 4:00 p.m. Be on time, if not a little early. If you come in late, find a seat and get ready to work. Don't interrupt the group to explain or apologize.
- If you know ahead of time that you'll be late or will miss a meeting, we appreciate it if you let at least one member of the group know so we're not wondering where you are, especially if your work is due to be critiqued.
- Attend every meeting if possible. You will not get any value out of the group if you only show up once in a while. Professionalism includes committing to full participation.
  - If you need help with transportation, say so. Carpooling is often an option.
  - Another option is to join the group via a video conferencing app. We currently use Zoom (https://zoom.us/download). With a little advance notice, this is easy to arrange. If your computer does not already have a webcam installed, you can buy one for around $50, and Zoom's basic services are free.

  Zoom
- We use the first part of each meeting for writing- or publishing-related announcements or information. Please share personal news before or after the meeting, or after all the work is done.
- Be considerate of the author and speaker: avoid starting side conversations, passing handwritten notes, texting, or reading your email. These distract other group members and mean you're missing what's being said. Remember, we learn by hearing what other members have to say about the work being critiqued, even when it's not our own. No, you can't multitask. Really.
- Work will be reviewed in the order of the meeting agenda, which is generally emailed to the group the Saturday before the meeting.

- Read and critique *all* the work that's submitted. While you should email your critique to the group, we expect every member of the group to provide substantive verbal critique during the meetings.
  - Substantive critique means staying on topic while you discuss problems with, or good points of, plot, characterization, setting, pacing, word choice, point of view, etc. Use the appropriate critique guide. We have guides for fiction and memoir, general nonfiction, creative nonfiction, and poetry. They will be provided separately.
  - Substantive critique does not include discussing typos, punctuation or page formatting errors, and the like unless they significantly confused you. These things should be noted in the manuscript.
  - If you have no substantive comments, or if yours have already been covered, say so and let the next reviewer speak.
- Make every effort to stay caught up with the work. While we schedule two meetings to discuss each piece, if you get behind and only get to it after the whole group has reviewed it, simply hand or send your marked-up copy to the author. If you feel you absolutely must discuss it, arrange a separate time to talk.
- Many new writers don't know how to critique. This is normal: it *is* a learned skill. These are the key things to know about critiquing.
  - Always discuss the work; never criticize the writer.
  - Be specific. Vague and generic statements like "Well, I liked it… " have no value. Try to explain why you liked or had problems with something. Suggest solutions, if possible, but do not insist that the writer rewrite their story your way. It's their story, not yours.
  - Critique is not only about the problems in a piece; authors need to hear what worked well too, and why. That said, don't worry about hurting someone's feelings by identifying problems. That's what we want, and we've learned to have thick skins.

- - There are many excellent resources available to help you learn how to critique.
    - Start by simply listening closely to what experienced group members say. Compare their comments to what you observed—or missed.
    - Group member Ross Lampert is currently writing several books on how to critique. The Craft & Critique series will be available from all the online book retailers when the series is published.
- Be sure to put your name on your critique and your name or initials in the filename of the copy you send back to the author. These help the author keep track of who said what in case they have questions later.

Submitting Your Work and Receiving Critique

- You *do not* have to submit work in order to be a valuable member of the group, or to learn from it, but your work will improve most if you do submit it.
- Writing is a craft; study it. New writers in particular have more to learn than they realize. Some group members have made books on writing from their collections available to be checked out. Feel free to borrow these books, but be sure to return them in a timely way.
- We expect you to already have a firm grasp on the basics of spelling, grammar, punctuation, and capitalization. If you do not, you are not ready for this group and we strongly recommend taking one or more classes to bring your skills up to the necessary level.
- Email your work to the group as an attachment. We prefer Rich Text Format (.rtf) or the current Microsoft Word format (.docx) but PDF is OK too. Information on how to do this and on recommended manuscript format is available separately.
- When you send out your work, give it a filename that clearly identifies the work or the author. For example, "Chapter 3.rtf" is too generic: the group may be working on several Chapter 3s at once.

- Include the genre and/or other significant information about the work in the cover email the first time you submit it if doing so will help the group understand what they're about to read, or will warn them about subject matter that might be a problem.
- If a work is complex, it may help to provide a map of the story world; a list of the characters with brief descriptions of their appearance, relationships, and roles; and/or brief descriptions of equipment, technologies, or supernatural phenomena. This is especially true for science fiction and fantasy.
- We allow you to respond while your work is being critiqued but ask you to limit what you say.
    - Do ask questions if you don't understand something a reviewer said.
    - Do not explain your work. If you need to explain it, or some element of it, it's not clear enough. Readers will not have the opportunity to ask you for explanations, so everything the reader needs to know must be on the page. That said, if you've intentionally left something unclear because you're setting up a future event, do explain that if necessary.
    - Spoilers are not relevant in a critique group. Group members need to know about future events to understand how the story will develop.
    - Do not be defensive about your work. It's not under attack and we're on your side! Our objective is to help you make your work the best it can be. This also prepares you for what will happen after your work has been published. Defending your work against online attackers will just draw more attacks. Writers need to have a thick skin, and this is the place to start growing it if needed.
- You *do not* have to take all reviewers' suggestions. For one thing, they may be contradictory! Use what makes sense to you. That said, do look for trends in our comments. If three or more of us said the same thing, that's a very strong sign there's a problem—or a real success.

Conclusion

Your work *will* get better if you actively participate in this group. We've seen it happen time after time. We look forward to seeing it happen with your work too.

THANK YOU AND PLEASE

Thank you for reading *Giving and Receiving Effective Critique*. I hope you enjoyed it, or it engaged you, challenged you, or at least made you think. Now I'd like to ask you to do one of the following things. I'd appreciate it if you signed up for my newsletter by filling in the form in the footer of my website's Home page (https://thecritiquedoctor.com). I also have a page on BookBub (https://www.bookbub.com/profile/ross-b-lampert) and a "follow" there would be terrific. Or tell one friend about the book. Just one!

The Critique Doctor

BookBub

Or leave a review on Goodreads (https://www.goodreads.com/book/show/240376548-giving-and-receiving-effective-critique), your favorite review site, or wherever you purchased this book. Your review doesn't have to be long, deep, or complex. No advanced degrees in literary criticism required! All I ask is that it's honest. I'll think you're wonderful if you leave that review, and so will others who are thinking about buying or borrowing the book.

Giving and Receiving Effective Critique
Goodreads

CONNECT WITH ME ONLINE

Web site: https://www.thecritiquedoctor.com
Facebook author page: https://www.facebook.com/profile.php?id=100082372310629
Amazon author page: https://amazon.com/author/ross_b_lampert
LinkedIn: https://www.linkedin.com/in/rblampert
Goodreads: https://www.goodreads.com/user/show/193743025-ross-lampert
BookBub: https://www.bookbub.com/profile/ross-b-lampert

The Critique Doctor

Facebook

Amazon

LinkedIn

Goodreads

BookBub

ABOUT THE AUTHOR

Ross Lampert, a.k.a. The Critique Doctor, has been writing since third grade, when the class performed his one-act play based on the Mercury space missions. He joined his first organized critique group while he was in college at the University of Colorado at Boulder.

While his writing and critiquing activity waxed and waned during his Air Force career, he got serious about both after he retired. He formed the Broncho[2] Writers' Group while getting his master's degree in English at the University of Central Oklahoma (UCO), and he's been writing and critiquing ever since.

After moving to Arizona in 2006, he joined one critique group, decided the way it worked wasn't for him, and formed the Cochise Writers' Group in 2007. That group is still going strong. Many of the group's current or former members have published short stories, poems, memoirs, or novels.

Along the way, Ross has learned a lot about what makes a good critique group and a good (effective, useful) critique—and what doesn't. He's happy to share that knowledge with you through The Critique Doctor website (https://thecritiquedoctor.com/) and this series.

The Critique Doctor

---

[2] That's how they spell bronco at UCO—don't ask me why.

WHAT'S IN THE REST OF THE SERIES

Book 0, Finding the Write Fit (https://books2read.com/u/mYO8wY) is a guide for evaluating one or more in-person critique groups, social media–based groups, or online critique sites to find one that's a good fit for you. It also provides an overview of online and in-person courses and classes that aren't associated with a college or university, looks at artificial intelligence applications as potential critique tools, and guides you through the process of forming your own in-person group if you decide you aren't comfortable with any of the other options.

Finding the Write Fit

Book 2, *Mechanics, Narrative, and Description* (https://books2read.com/u/4NOogJ), provides you with tools for evaluating an author's use of the mechanics of writing: spelling, grammar, punctuation, and capitalization. Then it digs into narrative, the text outside of quotation marks, and description, in setting, characterization, and other areas.

Mechanics, Narrative, and Description

Book 3, *Theme, Plot, and Structure* (https://books2read.com/u/mdOjqd), looks at those topics and much more: the beginnings and endings of scenes, chapters, and whole books; what theme, plot, and structure are and how they work together; how stakes, conflict, tension, and pace are woven into a story—or should be—and how to tell if the writer is handling all these topics well.

Theme, Plot, and Structure

Book 4, *Characters and Dialogue* (https://books2read.com/u/mYOzkM), covers all the aspects of the people or other beings who populate our books: their roles, how they're portrayed, and how they communicate with each other.

Book 5, *Poetry Critique for Prose Writers* (https://books2read.com/u/mB6QqN), will demystify the processes of reading, understanding, and critiquing poems. If you're a member of an in-person group, or join one later, it's a good bet that at some time you'll be asked to review someone's poetry. For many prose writers, this can be an intimidating request. This book will help you overcome that feeling. And who knows, you might even discover that you *like* poetry!

Characters and Dialogue

Poetry Critique for Prose Writers

OTHER BOOKS BY ROSS B. LAMPERT

The Eternity Plague series:

The Eternity Plague: https://books2read.com/u/3JMNzA
Chrysalis: https://books2read.com/u/bzNQEz
Wild Spread: https://books2read.com/u/3LMeP7

The Eternity Plague   Chrysalis   Wild Spread

www.ingramcontent.com/pod-product-compliance
Lightning Source LLC
Chambersburg PA
CBHW070100100426
42743CB00012B/2609